Letterland

ELT

Hello! I'm Monkey.
What's your name?

My name is

_____

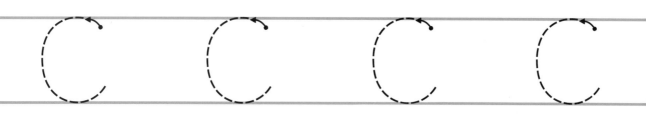

Clever Cat

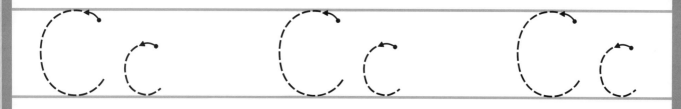

Trace over the correct number.

How many  ?

3

4

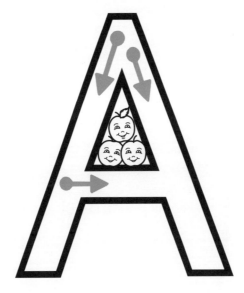

Annie Apple

A A A A A

Aa Aa Aa

Trace over the correct number.

How many 🍎 ?

1 2 3

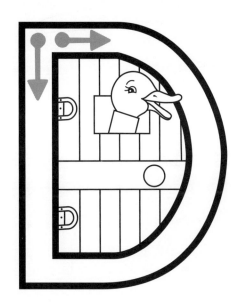

Dippy Duck

D D D D

Dd Dd Dd

Trace over the correct number.

How many 🦆 ? 1 2 3 4 5

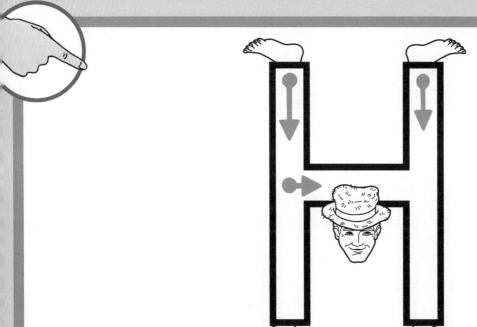

Harry Hat Man

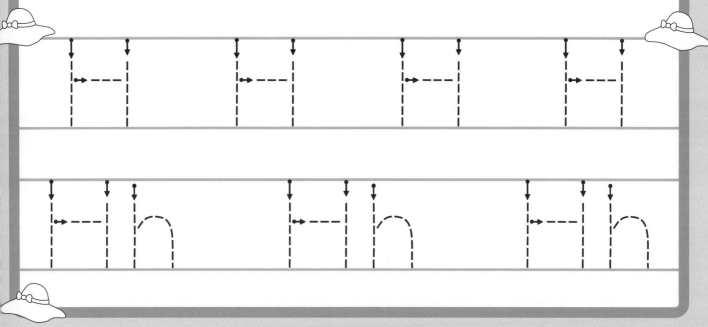

Trace over the correct number.

How many ? 1 2 3 4 5

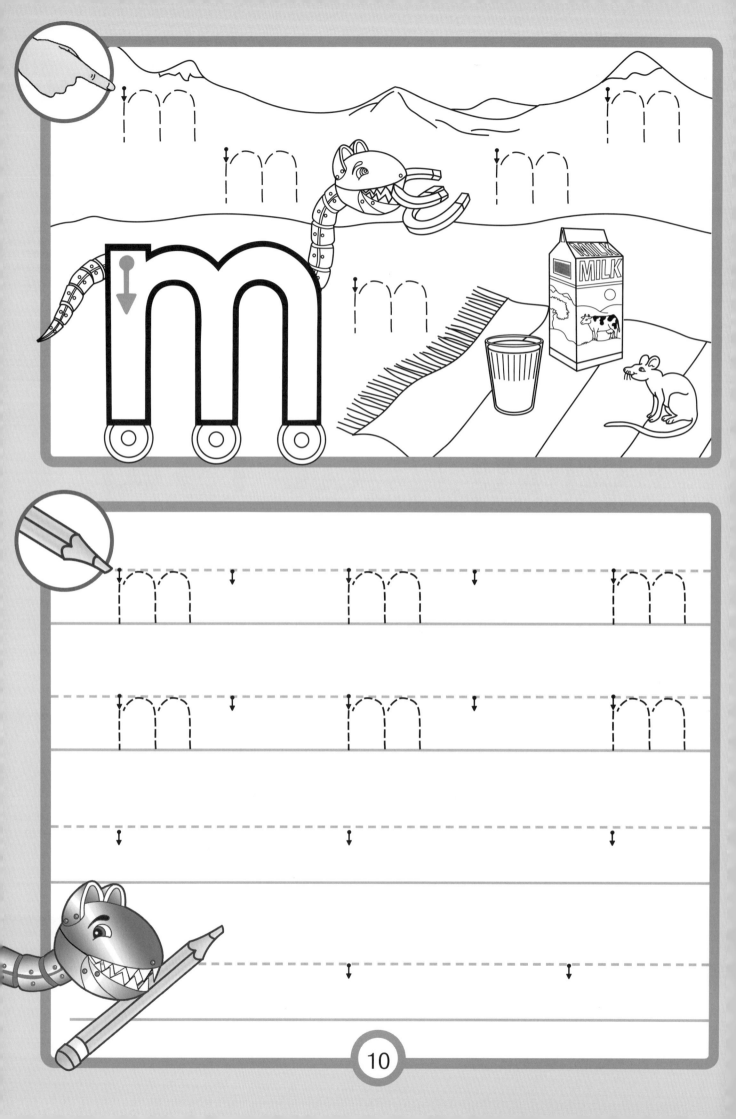

Munching Mike

M M M M

Mm Mm Mm

Trace over the correct number.

How many ? 1 2 3 4 5

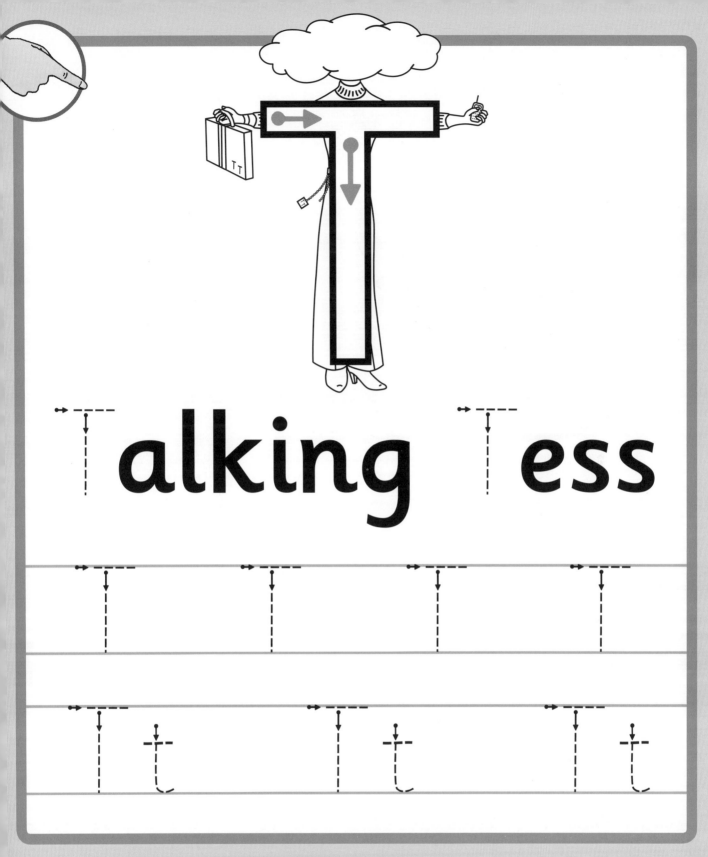

Talking Tess

T T T T

t t t

Count and trace over all the numbers.

Numbers 1 2 3 4 5

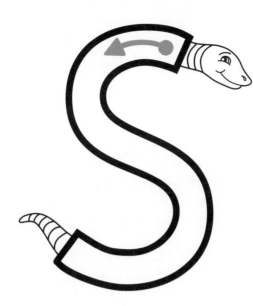

Sammy Snake

S S S S

S s S s S s S s

Count and trace over all the numbers.

Numbers 1 2 3 4 5

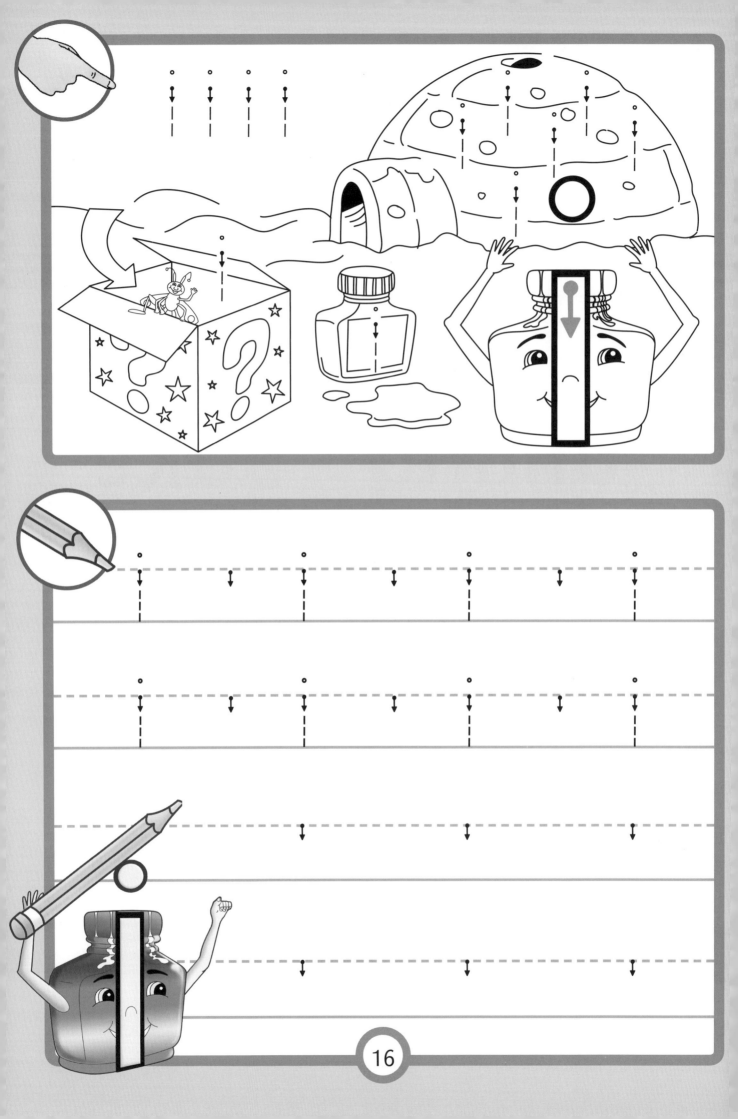

mpy nk

Count and trace over all the numbers.

Numbers

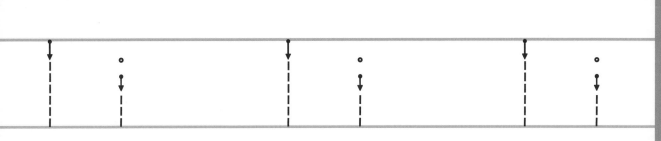

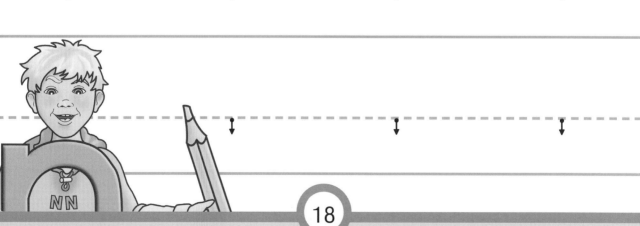

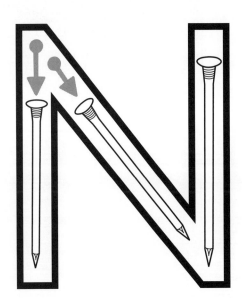

Noisy Nick

N N N N

Nn Nn Nn

Count and trace over all the numbers.

Numbers

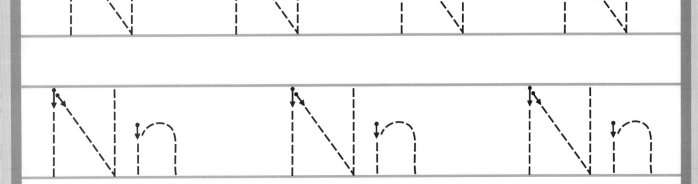

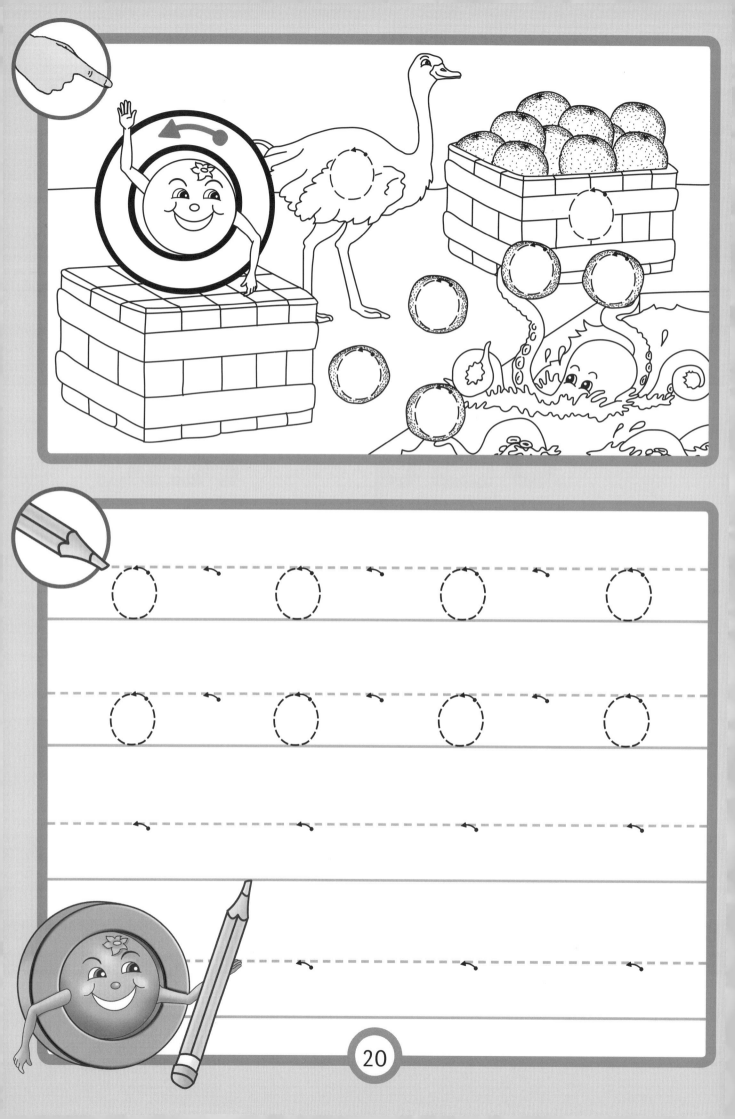

Oscar Orange

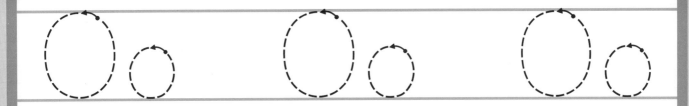

Count and trace over all the numbers.

Numbers

12345

Peter Puppy

P   P   P   P

P p   P p   P p

Count and trace over all the numbers.

Numbers

6789

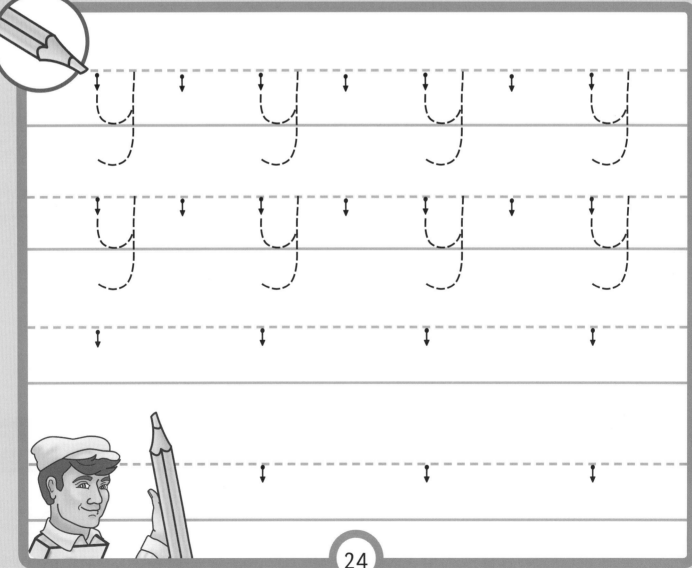

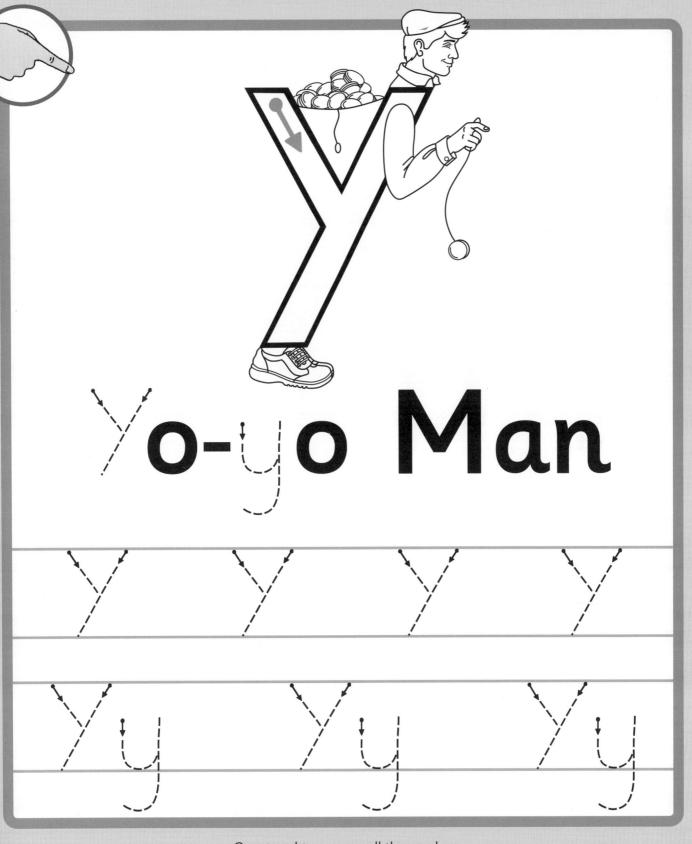

Yo-yo Man

Count and trace over all the numbers.

Numbers 6789

Golden Girl

Count and trace over all the numbers.

Numbers 6789

Eddy Elephant

Count and trace over all the numbers.

Numbers

6789

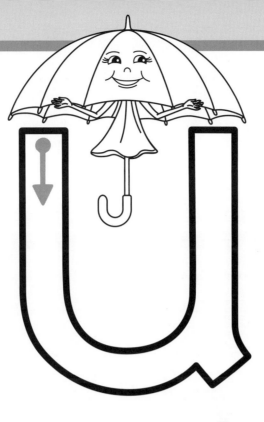

Uppy Umbrella

Count and trace over all the numbers.

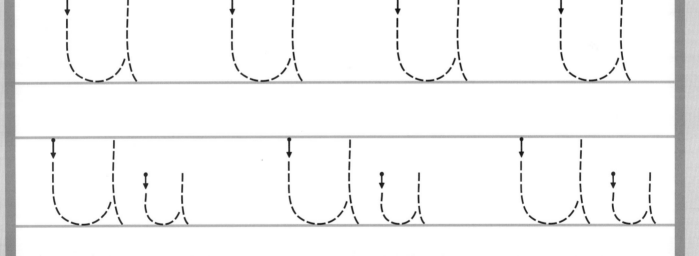

Numbers

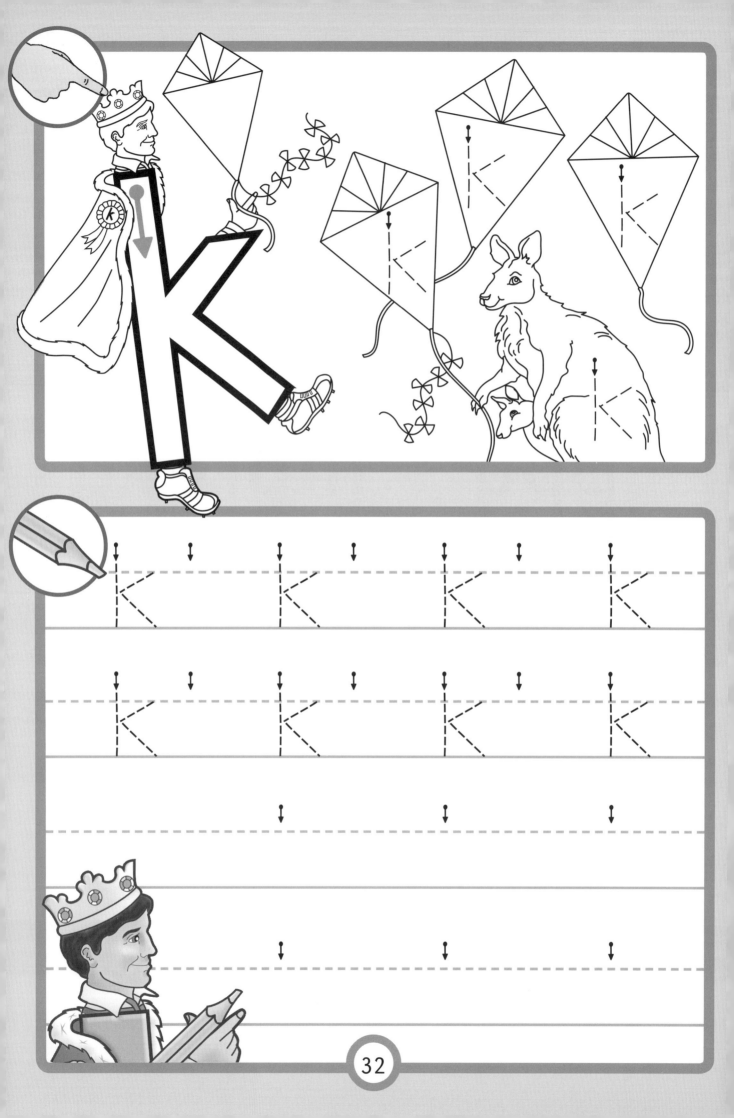

Kicking King

Count and trace over all the numbers.

123456789

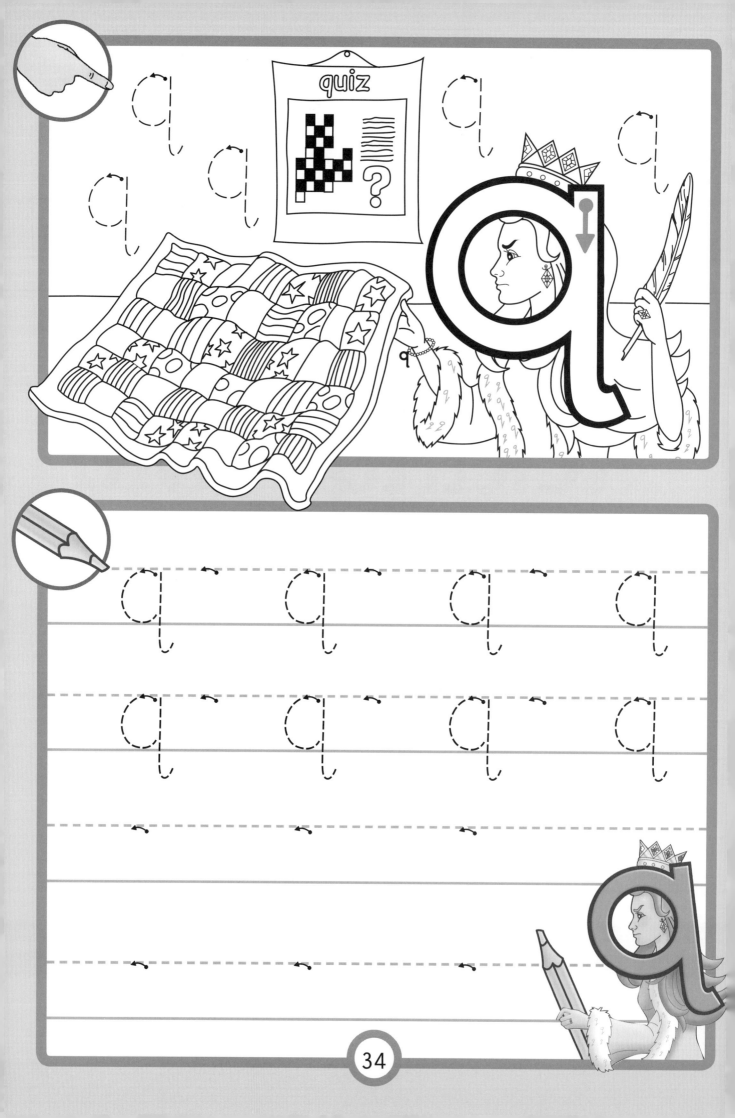

quiz

Quarrelsome Queen

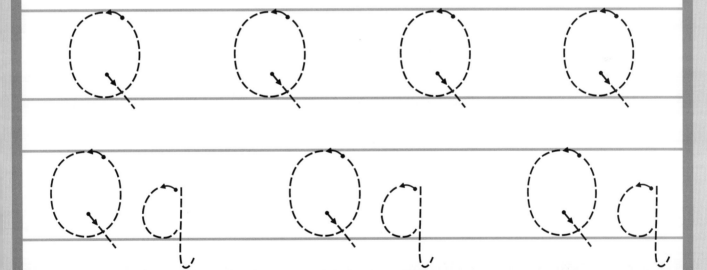

Count and trace over all the numbers.

123456789

Firefighter Fred

F F F F

f f f

Count and trace over all the numbers.

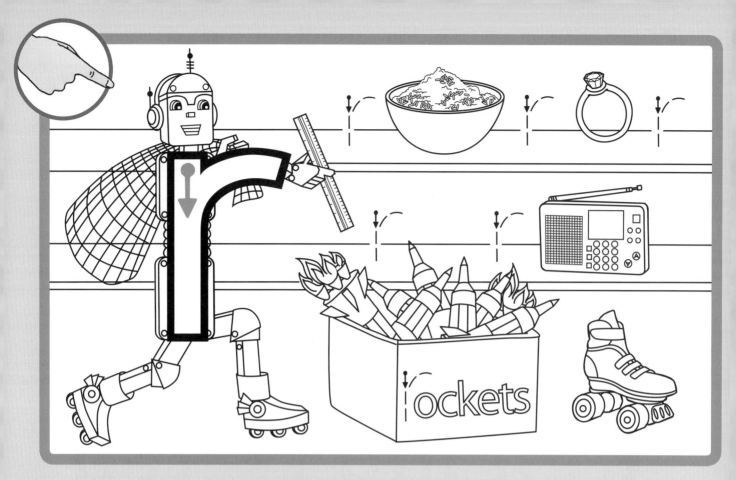

Red Robot

R R R R

R Rr R Rr R Rr

Count and trace over all the numbers.

1 2 3 4 5 6 7 8 9

Lucy Lamp Light

Count and trace over all the numbers.

123456789

Vicky Violet

Count and trace over all the numbers.

1 2 3 4 5 6 7 8 9

Jumping Jim

Count and trace over all the numbers.

1 2 3 4 5 6 7 8 9

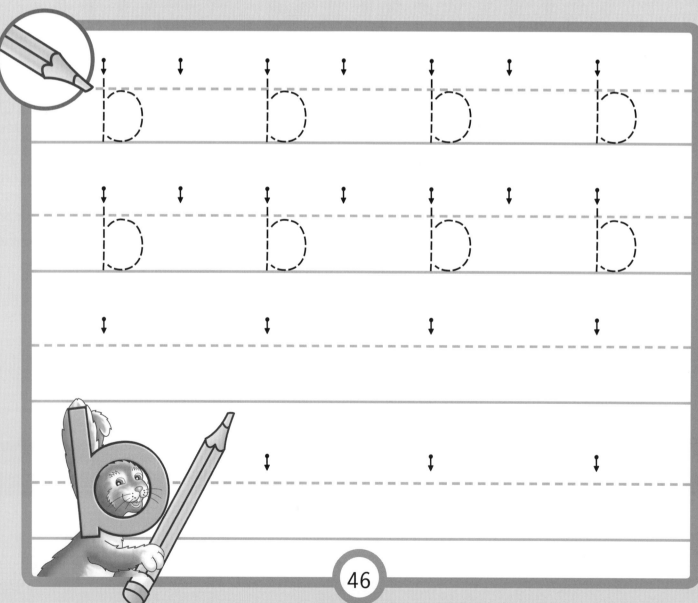

Bouncy Ben

B B B B

Bb Bb Bb Bb

Count and trace over all the numbers.

1 2 3 4 5 6 7 8 9

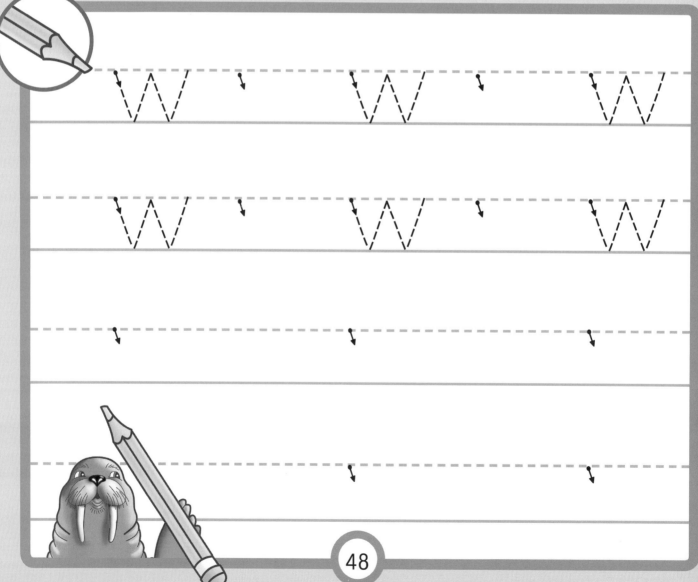

Walter Walrus

W W W W W

Ww Ww Ww Ww

Count and trace over all the numbers.

1 2 3 4 5 6 7 8 9

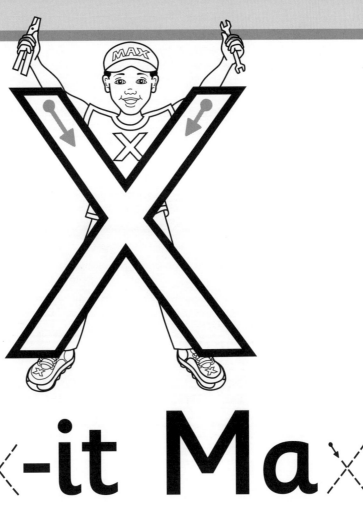

Fix-it Max

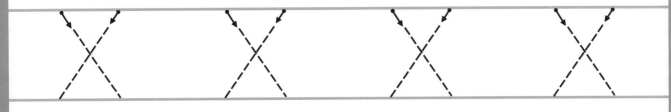

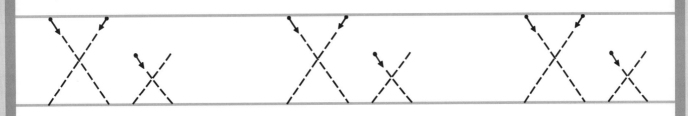

Count and trace over all the numbers.

1 2 3 4 5 6 7 8 9

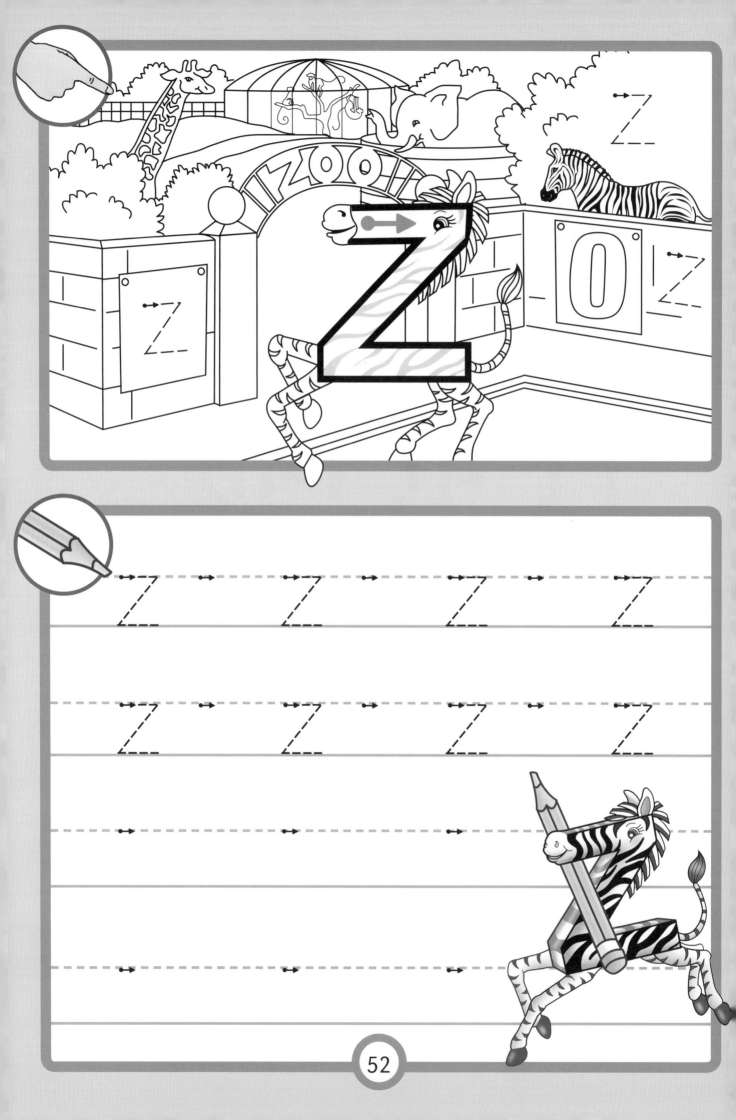

Zig Zag Zebra

Z Z Z Z

Z Z Z Z

Count and trace over all the numbers.

1 2 3 4 5 6 7 8 9

Handwriting Songs

Annie Apple

At the leaf begin.
Go round the apple this way.
Then add a line down,
so Annie won't roll away.

Bouncy Ben

Brush down Ben's
big, long ears.
Go up and round his head
so his face appears!

Clever Cat

Curve round Clever Cat's
face to begin.
Then gently tickle her
under her chin.

Dippy Duck

Draw Dippy Duck's back.
Go round her tum.
Go up to her head.
Then down you come!

Eddy Elephant

Ed has a headband.
Draw it and then
stroke round his head
and his trunk to the end.

Firefighter Fred

First draw Fred's helmet.
Then go down a way.
Give him some arms
and he'll put out the blaze.

Golden Girl

Go round Golden Girl's head.
Go down her golden hair.
Then curve to make her swing,
so she can sit there.

Harry Hat Man

Hurry from the Hat Man's head
down to his heel on the ground.
Go up and bend his knee over,
so he'll hop while he makes
his sound.

Impy Ink

Inside the ink bottle
draw a line.
Add an inky dot. That's fine!

Jumping Jim

Just draw down Jim,
bending his knees.
Then add the one ball
which everyone sees.

Kicking King

Kicking King's body
is a straight stick.
Add his arm, then his leg,
so he can kick!

Lucy Lamp Light

Lucy looks like
one long line.
Go straight from head to foot
and she's ready to shine!

Munching Mike

Make Munching Mike's
back leg first,
then his second leg,
and third,
so he can go munch-munching
in a word.

Noisy Nick

'Now bang my nail,'
Noisy Nick said.
'Go up and over
around my head.'

Oscar Orange

On Oscar Orange
start at the top.
Go all the way round him,
and... then stop.

Peter Puppy

Pat Peter Puppy properly.
First stroke down his ear,
then up and round his face
so he won't shed a tear.

Quarrelsome Queen

Quickly go round the
Queen's cross face.
Then comb her beautiful
hair into place.

Red Robot

Run down Red Robot's body.
Go up to his arm
and his hand.
Then watch out for this robot
roaming round Letterland.

Sammy Snake

Start at Sam's head
where he can see.
Stroke down to his tail,
oh so care-ful-ly!

Talking Tess

Tall as a tower make
Talking Tess stand.
Go from head to toe,
and then from hand to hand.

Uppy Umbrella

Under the umbrella
draw a shape like a cup.
Then draw a straight line
so it won't tip up.

Vicky Violet

Very neatly, start at the top.
Draw down your vase,
then up and stop.

Walter Walrus

When you draw the
Walrus wells,
with wild and wavy water,
whizz down and up
and then...,
whizz down and up again.

Fix-it Max

Fix two sticks, to look like this.
That's how to draw a little kiss.

Yo-yo Man

You first make the yo-yo sack
on the Yo-yo Man's back,
and then go down to his toes
so he can sell his yo-yos.

Zig Zag Zebra

Zip along Zig Zag's nose.
Stroke her neck...,
stroke her back...
Zzzoom! Away she goes.

These songs are
available on CD see
www.letterland.com

Letterland ELT

The Letterland ELT range includes:

- ✔ Letterland ELT Teacher's Guide
- ✔ Letterland ELT Student Book
- ✔ Letterland ELT Student Book CD
- ✔ Letterland ELT Workbook
- ✔ Letterland ELT Handwriting Book

- ✔ Letterland ELT Alphabet Songs
- ✔ Vocabulary Cards
- ✔ Big Picture Code Cards
- ✔ Alphabet Frieze

Teacher's Guide
by Gudrun Freese

Student Book

Workbook

Handwriting

Student Book CD

cake

a

Alphabet Songs CD